3474    9431

# Find It on the
# FARM

## Dee Phillips

GARETH**STEVENS**
PUBLISHING
A Member of the WRC Media Family of Companies

Please visit our web site at: **www.garethstevens.com**
For a free color catalog describing Gareth Stevens Publishing's list of high-quality books and multimedia programs, call 1-800-542-2595 (USA) or 1-800-387-3178 (Canada). Gareth Stevens Publishing's fax: (414) 332-3567.

Library of Congress Cataloging-in-Publication Data

Phillips, Dee, 1967-
    Find it on the farm / by Dee Phillips.
      p. cm. — (Can you find it?)
    ISBN 0-8368-6303-8 (lib. bdg.)
    1. Domestic animals—Juvenile literature. I. Title.
  SF75.5.P45   2006
  636—dc22                 2005030341

This North American edition first published in 2006 by
**Gareth Stevens Publishing**
A Member of the WRC Media Family of Companies
330 West Olive Street, Suite 100
Milwaukee, WI 53212 USA

This U.S. edition copyright © 2006 by Gareth Stevens, Inc. Original edition copyright © 2005 by ticktock Entertainment Ltd. First published in Great Britain in 2005 by ticktock Media Ltd., Unit 2, Orchard Business Centre, North Farm Road, Tunbridge Wells, Kent TN2 3XF.

Gareth Stevens series editor: Dorothy L. Gibbs
Gareth Stevens graphic designer: Charlie Dahl
Gareth Stevens art direction: Tammy West

Picture credits: (t=top, b=bottom, l=left, r=right, c=center)
Alamy: 4-5. FLPA: 4-5, 6-7c, 10-11c, 13, 14l, 17, 19, 20.
Every effort has been made to trace the copyright holders for the pictures used in this book. We apologize in advance for any unintentional omissions and would be pleased to insert the appropriate acknowledgements in any subsequent edition.

Printed in the United States of America

1 2 3 4 5 6 7 8 9 10 09 08 07 06

Words that appear in the glossary are printed in **boldface** type the first time they occur in the text.

# Contents

# The Farm

**T**here is so much to see on the farm, from horses, cows, sheep, and other animals to the farmer and the **machinery** that helps him do his work.

# What can you find on the farm?

Horse

Hay

Cows

Rooster

Ducks

Sheep

Tractor

Sheepdog

Donkey

# Horse

**H**orses live on lots of farms. They are used to **herd** animals and to do heavy work, such as pulling wagons. Farmers may also raise horses for riding or racing.

A female horse is called a mare. A baby horse is called a foal. A male horse is called a stallion.

Horses like to eat hay, juicy grass, and other kinds of plants.

Horses feet are called hooves. Some farmers put metal "shoes" on their horses' feet to **protect** the hooves from **damage**.

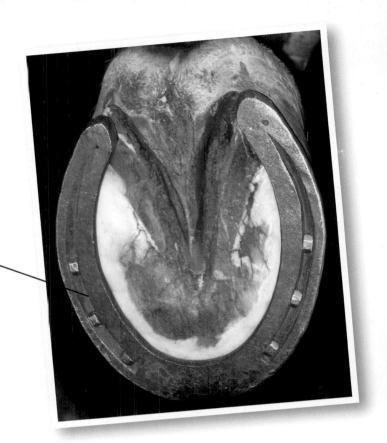

A Shire horse is a tall, strong animal with fluffy white feet. In the past, Shire horses were used to pull wagons and to plow fields.

# Hay

Hay is made from dried grass.  Farmers use hay to feed their animals during winter, when there is often no fresh grass for them to **graze** on.

Farmers make bundles of hay called bales.  Bales of hay are easier for farmers to carry than loose hay would be.

Bales of hay are piled on top of each other to make **haystacks**. Haystacks are like food stores for farm animals.

Late in summer, when the grass is tall, machines cut, or mow, it down. Mowing the tall grass is called **harvesting**. After the grass is harvested, it is left out in the sun to dry into hay.

# Cows

The cows on a farm live together in a herd. Cows that are raised to give milk live on dairy farms.

A farmer may keep only a few cows on his farm or a herd of dozens.

Milk comes from the **udder** of a female cow, which is between her back legs.

Cows can drink about a bathtub full of water a day.

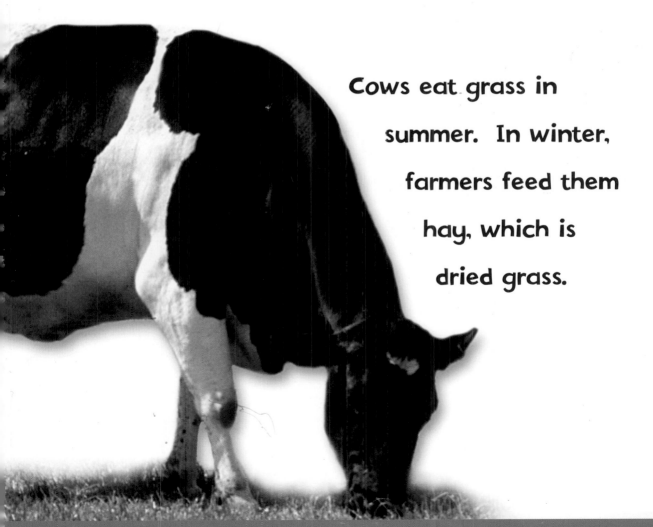

Cows eat grass in summer. In winter, farmers feed them hay, which is dried grass.

# Rooster

A rooster is a male chicken. When the Sun comes up each morning, a rooster makes a sound like "cock-a-doodle-doo."

A rooster has a large **comb** on the top of his head.

Roosters look after all the female chickens on the farm.

The loud screeching sound a rooster makes is called a "crow." Crowing is one of the ways a rooster marks its territory.

# Ducks

Ducks are birds that live on or near water. They have **webbed** feet, which help them swim. Many ducks live on farmyard ponds.

Ducks make their nests near water. A female duck will lay up to twelve eggs in her nest. The eggs will hatch into baby ducks, or ducklings.

Ducklings
learn how
to swim
by copying
their parents.

Ducks fly only part of the year.

Their flight feathers fall out every July.

They hide in **reeds** for about six weeks until the

feathers have grown back.

# Sheep

Farmers have raised sheep for thousands of years. These animals are known for their soft, thick coats of curly or shaggy wool.

Every year, the farmer cuts off, or shears, a sheep's wool. The wool is sold to make yarn for sweaters, coats, and rugs.

A female sheep is called a ewe. Baby sheep are called lambs.

Lambs are born in springtime. They drink their mother's milk for about three months. Then, they are old enough to graze on grass and other plants.

# Tractor

**M**ost farmers use tractors to help them do their work. These large machines are good for farming because they can pull heavy loads.

A tractor's big, strong wheels help keep it from getting stuck in soft ground.

Farmers use tractors for tasks such as making hay or harvesting **crops**.

Tractors are used to pull many other kinds of machines. This machine is called a harvester.

# Sheepdog

A sheepdog's main job is to round up sheep. Farmers train sheepdogs to understand special whistles that tell the dogs what to do.

Sheepdogs are a special breed of dogs. The name of the breed is border collie. These dogs are known to be intelligent and **obedient**.

Farmers teach sheepdogs to round up sheep and herd them into pens.

A sheepdog herds sheep by **crouching** close to the ground and **stalking** the sheep without taking its eyes off the flock.

21

# Donkey

onkeys are members of the horse family. They are strong, but gentle, and have many uses.

Farmers use donkeys to carry loads, to protect sheep and other farm animals, and to keep nervous horses company.

Donkeys have long ears and short, stiff **manes**. Their tails end in tufts of dark hair.

A donkey has a very **distinctive** voice! It makes a rasping, or grating, noise that sounds like "hee-haw."

# Glossary

**comb** – the red skinlike crest on top of a chicken's head

**crops** – plants that are grown for food or the materials to make things

**crouching** – bending down low and close to the ground

**damage** – harm or injury

**distinctive** – easy to recognize

**graze** – to feed on grass and other plants in a field

**harvesting** – cutting down crops that are fully grown

**haystacks** – bales of hay that are piled up for storage

**herd** – (n) a group of animals that stay together most of the time (v) to gather a group of animals together

**machinery** – mechanical or motorized equipment that does work people used to have to do with hand tools

**manes** – strips of hair that grow down the heads and necks of horses, donkeys, or other similar animals

**obedient** – following orders or commands

**plow** – to turn over the ground to make it ready for planting crops

**protect** – to keep safe from harm

**reeds** – tall, thin stalks of grasslike plants that grow in or near a pond, lake, or river

**stalking** – following someone or something closely and for a long time, sometimes to do harm

**udder** – the part of a cow where the milk comes out

**webbed** – joined together with skin, like the toes on a duck's or a frog's feet